Chapter 1: Introduction to Reasonable Adjustments

Definition and Purpose

Reasonable adjustments are changes or modifications made to educational practices, environments, or resources to ensure that all students, particularly those with disabilities, can participate fully in their education. These adjustments aim to remove or reduce barriers that students with special educational needs (SEN) might face, ensuring they have equal opportunities to succeed.

The purpose of reasonable adjustments is to create an inclusive educational environment where all students, regardless of their physical, sensory, cognitive, or emotional needs, can access and benefit from the same educational opportunities. This involves tailoring support to individual needs without compromising academic standards.

Legal Framework: Equality Act 2010

The Equality Act 2010 is a comprehensive piece of legislation in the UK that aims to protect individuals from discrimination and promote equality. Under this Act, educational institutions are legally required to make reasonable adjustments for students with disabilities.

Key points of the Equality Act 2010 relevant to education include:

- **Duty to Make Adjustments**: Schools and colleges must take reasonable steps to avoid putting disabled students at a substantial disadvantage compared to their non-disabled peers.

- **Three Requirements**:

  - *Provision, Criterion, or Practice*: Adjusting policies, practices, or procedures that may disadvantage disabled students.

  - *Physical Features*: Making physical changes to the environment to ensure accessibility.

  - *Auxiliary Aids*: Providing additional support or aids, such as assistive technology, to help disabled students access education.

Importance in Education Settings

Implementing reasonable adjustments is crucial in education settings for several reasons:

Equity and Inclusion: Ensures that all students, regardless of their abilities, have access to education and can participate fully.

Legal Compliance: Adhering to the Equality Act 2010 and other relevant legislation helps institutions avoid legal repercussions.

Academic Success: Tailoring support to individual needs helps students overcome barriers to learning, leading to better educational outcomes.

Positive School Culture: Promoting inclusivity and diversity fosters a supportive and respectful school environment.

Social and Emotional Development: Inclusive practices help students develop social skills, self-esteem, and a sense of belonging.

OVERVIEW OF THE BOOKLET

This booklet aims to provide educators with comprehensive guidance on implementing reasonable adjustments within their schools or colleges. It covers the following areas:

- **Legal and Regulatory Framework**: Detailed exploration of the Equality Act 2010, SEND Regulations 2014, and other relevant legislation.

- **Being Preemptive**: Strategies for early identification of needs and collaboration with parents, carers, and primary school feeder settings.

- **Understanding Protected Characteristics**: Explanation of protected characteristics and their impact on students.

- **Implementing Support in the Classroom**: Practical strategies for differentiated instruction, use of assistive technology, and creating an inclusive classroom culture.

- **Making Reasonable Adjustments**: Identifying specific needs and providing practical examples of adjustments in various educational contexts.

- **Normal Way of Working and Access Arrangements for Examinations**: Understanding and implementing access arrangements in line with JCQ guidelines.

- **Supporting Students with Medical Needs**: Best practices for managing and supporting students with medical needs, including creating individual healthcare plans and staff training.

Chapter 2: Legal and Regulatory Frameworks

EQUALITY ACT 2010

The Equality Act 2010 is a comprehensive piece of legislation in the UK designed to consolidate and streamline previous anti-discrimination laws. Its primary aim is to protect individuals from unfair treatment and promote a fairer and more equal society. This section will explore the key aspects of the Equality Act 2010 relevant to education, focusing on reasonable adjustments for students with disabilities.

Key Provisions of the Equality Act 2010

The Act identifies several protected characteristics, including disability, defined as a physical or mental impairment that has a substantial and long-term adverse effect on a person's ability to carry out normal day-to-day activities. One of the central tenets of the Act is the duty to make reasonable adjustments, ensuring that disabled students are not at a substantial disadvantage compared to their non-disabled peers.

Reasonable adjustments are required in three main areas: provision, criterion, or practice (PCP); physical features; and auxiliary aids. Adjustments to PCP involve modifying teaching methods or assessment procedures that might otherwise disadvantage disabled students. For physical features, schools may need to alter the environment to ensure accessibility, such as installing ramps or lifts. Providing auxiliary aids includes offering support or aids like hearing loops, adapted keyboards, or other assistive technologies.

An important aspect of this duty is its anticipatory nature, meaning that schools must consider and plan for the needs of disabled students in advance, rather than waiting for specific needs to arise. This proactive approach requires institutions to be vigilant in identifying potential barriers and addressing them before they impact students.

The Act also prohibits direct and indirect discrimination. Direct discrimination occurs when a person is treated less favourably because of their disability, while indirect discrimination happens when a PCP is applied equally to all but disadvantages a person with a disability. Schools must ensure their policies and practices do not inadvertently discriminate against disabled students. Additionally, the Act protects students from harassment related to their disability and from victimisation if they make or support a complaint under the Act.

Implementing the Equality Act 2010 in Schools

To comply with the Equality Act 2010, schools must develop comprehensive policies that reflect their commitment to equality and inclusion. These policies should outline the school's approach to making reasonable adjustments, promoting inclusivity, and handling complaints of discrimination or harassment. All staff, including teachers, support staff, and administrative personnel, should receive training on the Act and its implications for their work. This training should cover identifying and addressing potential barriers for disabled students and implementing reasonable adjustments.

Inclusive curriculum design is another critical component. Schools should ensure that teaching materials and methods cater to diverse learning needs by using various teaching styles, incorporating assistive technology, and ensuring all students can access learning resources. Adjustments to the physical environment are also essential. Schools should conduct accessibility audits to identify potential barriers and make necessary adjustments, such as installing ramps or modifying classroom layouts.

Auxiliary aids and services play a significant role in supporting disabled students. Schools should provide a range of aids and services, such as sign language interpreters, speech-to-text software, or personal support assistants, to help these students access education effectively.

Case Studies and Examples

Consider a secondary school that identified difficulties for students with mobility impairments in accessing upper floors. In response, the school installed a lift and made classroom adjustments to ensure all classes could be held in accessible rooms when needed. This proactive measure ensured that all students could participate fully in school activities.

Another example is an FE college that recognised challenges faced by students with dyslexia in traditional lecture formats. The college introduced various assistive technologies, such as text-to-speech software, and provided lecture notes in advance. This enabled students to prepare and participate more effectively in lessons.

A primary school conducted regular training sessions for staff on supporting students with various disabilities. This included training on using auxiliary aids, recognising signs of different disabilities, and understanding the legal requirements of the Equality Act 2010. As a result, staff were better equipped to identify and address the needs of disabled students, creating a more inclusive learning environment.

Monitoring and Reviewing Adjustments

Regular reviews of policies and practices are crucial to ensure that schools meet their legal obligations under the Equality Act 2010. This might involve gathering feedback from students, parents, and staff, and making adjustments as necessary. Collecting and analysing data on the experiences and outcomes of disabled students can help schools identify areas for improvement. This data can inform policy development and ensure that reasonable adjustments are effective.

Involving students and parents in discussions about reasonable adjustments provides valuable insights and ensures that the adjustments meet the students' needs. Regular meetings and feedback sessions can facilitate this involvement.

SEND (Special Educational Needs and Disabilities) Regulations 2014

The SEND Regulations 2014 were introduced as part of a broader reform to improve the support provided to children and young people with special educational needs and disabilities (SEND) in England. These regulations emphasise a coordinated, person-centred approach to assessment and provision, ensuring that young people with SEND have access to the same opportunities as their peers.

Central to these regulations is the introduction of Education, Health, and Care (EHC) plans, which replace the previous Statements of Special Educational Needs. EHC plans are designed to provide a more integrated and holistic approach to supporting children and young people from birth to 25 years old. These plans identify the educational, health, and social care needs of the individual and outline the support required to meet those needs.

Teachers' Responsibilities Under the SEND Regulations

The SEND Regulations 2014 make it clear that teachers are responsible for the progress of all students, including those with SEN. Teachers are required to adhere to the provisions outlined in EHC plans and cannot selectively implement only parts of these plans.

Teachers are charged with delivering high-quality, inclusive education. This includes differentiating their teaching methods to accommodate the diverse needs of all students, ensuring that lesson plans and classroom activities are accessible. Teachers must implement all specified support, accommodations, and interventions outlined in the EHC plan, working collaboratively with the SENCO and other support staff to ensure full application of the plan's provisions.

In addition to implementing EHC plans, teachers are responsible for regularly monitoring the progress of students with SEN. This involves ongoing assessment and evaluation to ensure that students are making expected progress towards their individual goals. Teachers must maintain detailed records of these assessments and report any concerns or issues to the SENCO or other relevant staff.

The SEND Regulations also emphasise the importance of involving parents and carers in the educational process. Teachers must communicate regularly with families, providing updates on the student's progress and discussing any adjustments or additional support that may be needed. This partnership helps ensure that the student's needs are being met both at school and at home.

To effectively support students with SEN, teachers must engage in continuous professional development. This includes training on inclusive teaching practices, understanding specific disabilities, and learning how to implement EHC plans effectively. Schools are responsible for providing opportunities for such professional development to ensure that all staff are equipped to meet their legal obligations.

Consider a secondary school that identified a student with complex needs requiring coordinated support across education, health, and social care. The school worked with the local authority to conduct an EHC needs assessment, involving the student's family and relevant professionals. The resulting EHC plan provided a tailored package of support, including specialised teaching, therapy sessions, and social care assistance. Teachers implemented all aspects of the EHC plan, which significantly improved the student's educational experience and well-being.

Another example from a primary school highlights the effectiveness of a dedicated SENCO. This SENCO implemented a rigorous system for identifying and supporting students with SEND. Regular training sessions for staff ensured they were equipped to identify needs early and provide appropriate interventions. Teachers in this school proactively applied the provisions of EHC plans, resulting in improved outcomes for students with SEND and positive feedback from parents.

Educational institutions are required to regularly monitor and review the provision for students with SEND to ensure it remains effective and relevant. This involves collecting and analysing data on student progress, gathering feedback from students and parents, and making necessary adjustments to support strategies. Annual reviews of EHC plans provide an opportunity to evaluate progress, set new targets, and update the support plan as needed.

CHILDREN AND FAMILIES ACT 2014

The Children and Families Act 2014 is a comprehensive piece of legislation in the UK that significantly reformed the framework for supporting children and young people with special educational needs and disabilities (SEND). This Act aims to provide a more integrated and person-centred approach to SEND provision, ensuring that children and young people receive the support they need to achieve their potential.

The Children and Families Act 2014 introduced several key changes to the way SEND support is provided, focusing on improving outcomes for children and young people with SEND through a more holistic and coordinated approach.

Education, Health, and Care Plans (EHC Plans)

One of the most significant changes introduced by the Act is the replacement of Statements of Special Educational Needs with Education, Health, and Care (EHC) plans. EHC plans are designed to be more comprehensive, covering educational, health, and social care needs in a single document. These plans apply to individuals from birth up to the age of 25, ensuring continuity of support throughout education and into adulthood.

Person-Centred Approach

The Act places a strong emphasis on a person-centred approach, ensuring that the views, wishes, and feelings of the child or young person, and their family, are central to the planning and provision of support. This approach aims to empower families and involve them in decision-making processes.

Local Offer

Local authorities are required to publish a 'local offer' detailing the support and services available for children and young people with SEND in their area. The local offer provides information on education, health, and social care services, helping families understand what support they can expect and how to access it.

Joint Commissioning

The Act mandates joint commissioning of services by local authorities and health bodies. This means that education, health, and social care services must work together to plan and deliver integrated support for children and young people with SEND. Joint commissioning aims to ensure that services are better coordinated and meet the holistic needs of the individual.

Mediation and Dispute Resolution

To resolve disagreements between families and local authorities or schools, the Act introduces mediation services. These services provide a means of resolving disputes in a less formal and adversarial manner, promoting collaborative solutions.

Responsibilities of Schools and Teachers

The Children and Families Act 2014 reinforces the responsibility of schools and teachers to support all students, including those with SEND. Teachers are expected to provide high-quality, inclusive teaching that meets the diverse needs of their students. This includes differentiating instruction, implementing EHC plans, and working collaboratively with parents and professionals.

Teachers are integral to the successful implementation of EHC plans. They must ensure that the support outlined in the plans is provided, and that students with SEND can access the curriculum and participate fully in school life. Regular monitoring and assessment of student progress are essential, and teachers must adapt their teaching strategies based on these assessments.

Additionally, schools must provide regular training for staff to ensure they are equipped with the skills and knowledge to support students with SEND effectively. This professional development is crucial for maintaining a high standard of inclusive education.

A case study from a secondary school highlights the implementation of an EHC plan for a student with autism. The plan included specific strategies for managing sensory sensitivities and social interactions, as well as tailored academic support. Teachers received training on autism awareness and strategies for inclusive teaching. By following the EHC plan, the school was able to provide a supportive learning environment, resulting in improved academic and social outcomes for the student.

Another example from a primary school demonstrates the importance of the local offer. A family moving to a new area used the local authority's local offer to identify a primary school with strong support for students with dyslexia. The local offer provided detailed information on the school's resources and staff expertise, helping the family make an informed decision. The school then worked closely with the family to develop an

EHC plan, ensuring that the student received the necessary support from the start.

The Children and Families Act 2014 requires regular reviews of EHC plans to ensure they remain relevant and effective. These reviews involve evaluating the student's progress, setting new targets, and updating the support plan as needed. Schools must work closely with families and other professionals during these reviews to ensure that the provision continues to meet the student's needs.

In addition to EHC plan reviews, schools are expected to continuously monitor the effectiveness of their SEND provision. This includes gathering feedback from students and parents, analysing outcomes, and making necessary adjustments to support strategies. By doing so, schools can create a dynamic and responsive support system that promotes the success and well-being of all students.

MENTAL CAPACITY ACT 2005

The Mental Capacity Act 2005 (MCA) is a crucial piece of legislation in the UK that establishes a framework for making decisions on behalf of individuals who lack the capacity to make certain decisions for themselves. While it is often associated with adult care, the MCA is also highly relevant for young people over the age of 16, including those in post-16 education settings. This section outlines the key provisions of the MCA and their implications for supporting young people with special educational needs and disabilities (SEND) in further education (FE) and higher education (HE).

The MCA defines mental capacity as the ability to make a particular decision at the time it needs to be made. A person is considered to lack capacity if they are unable to understand, retain, or use the information relevant to the decision, or if they are unable to communicate their decision. The Act is underpinned by five key principles which guide its application.

Firstly, every adult has the right to make their own decisions and must be assumed to have capacity unless it is proven otherwise. This principle emphasises the importance of respecting individual autonomy. Secondly, individuals have the right to make decisions that others may consider unwise, as long as they have the capacity to do so. This principle recognises that freedom includes the possibility of making choices that others might not agree with.

Thirdly, individuals must be given all practicable help before anyone concludes that they cannot make their own decisions. This principle requires that support and information be provided to help individuals make decisions independently wherever possible. Fourthly, any decision made or action taken on behalf of a person who lacks capacity must be made in their best interests. This involves considering the individual's past and present wishes, feelings, beliefs, and values. Family members and other relevant parties should be consulted to ensure that decisions are made in a holistic and informed manner.

Finally, the least restrictive option principle dictates that anything done for or on behalf of a person who lacks capacity should be the least restrictive of their basic rights and freedoms. This principle aims to ensure that any intervention is proportionate and minimally intrusive.

In post-16 education settings, such as colleges and universities, it is crucial to support young people with SEND in making decisions about their education and future. This includes decisions about course selection, support services, accommodation, and personal care. Educators and support staff must be aware of the procedures for assessing capacity, which involves determining whether the young person can understand, retain, and use the information necessary to make a specific decision, and whether they can communicate their decision.

For young people who lack capacity, education providers must develop individualised support plans that reflect the principles of the MCA. These plans should outline the necessary support to enable the student to participate in their education as fully as possible and make decisions to the best of their ability. Schools and colleges should work closely with families, carers, and Independent Mental Capacity Advocates (IMCAs) where applicable to ensure that the best interests of the student are at the forefront of any decisions made on their behalf. This collaborative approach ensures that the student's needs, wishes, and rights are respected and upheld.

A case study from a college highlights the implementation of the MCA for a student with a learning disability who was unable to make decisions about their course of study. The college, in collaboration with the student's family and an IMCA, developed a support plan that included regular reviews and tailored learning activities designed to maximise the student's participation and learning outcomes. The plan also included strategies for helping the student make smaller, day-to-day decisions, thereby promoting their autonomy as much as possible.

Another example involves a young adult in a university setting who required decisions to be made about their accommodation due to severe anxiety and a lack of capacity to decide. The university worked with the student's mental health team, their family, and an IMCA to explore the best options for accommodation. The chosen solution ensured that the student's well-being and educational needs were met in the least restrictive manner.

Regular monitoring and review are crucial to ensure that decisions made under the MCA continue to reflect the best interests of the young person. Educational institutions should establish procedures for regularly reviewing support plans and decisions, involving the young person, their family, and any advocates in the process. This helps ensure that the support provided remains relevant and effective, adapting to any changes in the young person's needs or circumstances.

By understanding and implementing the provisions of the Mental Capacity Act 2005, schools and colleges can better support young people with SEND in making informed decisions about their education and future. This approach not only helps institutions meet their legal obligations but also promotes a more inclusive and supportive educational environment.

Chapter 3: Being Preemptive: Early Identification and Intervention

IMPORTANCE OF EARLY IDENTIFICATION

Early identification of special educational needs (SEN) is crucial for providing timely and effective support to students. Recognising and addressing these needs as soon as possible can significantly improve educational outcomes and overall well-being. Early intervention helps prevent the escalation of learning difficulties, behavioural issues, and emotional distress, enabling students to achieve their full potential in a supportive environment.

In secondary and further education (FE) settings, early identification is particularly important as it helps ensure that students transitioning from primary school receive the necessary support without delay. This continuity of care is essential for maintaining progress and building on previous interventions. For primary schools, early identification lays the foundation for effective support throughout a child's educational journey.

Methods for Identifying Needs Without Formal Diagnosis

Identifying needs without waiting for a formal diagnosis is essential for timely intervention. Teachers and support staff can use various methods to recognize and address students' needs early on. Observational assessments play a critical role in this process. By closely monitoring students' behaviour, engagement, and performance, educators can identify potential issues that may indicate underlying SEN.

Standardised screening tools and checklists can also be useful for identifying learning difficulties, behavioural issues, and emotional needs. These tools help create a structured approach to observing and recording signs of SEN, enabling educators to make informed decisions about further assessments and interventions.

Another effective method is to gather information from multiple sources, including parents, previous teachers, and other professionals who have worked with the student. This holistic approach ensures that all aspects of the student's development and behaviour are considered, providing a comprehensive understanding of their needs.

The Role of Observational Assessments

Observational assessments are a key component of early identification. These assessments involve systematically observing and recording students' behaviours, interactions, and performance in various settings, such as the classroom, playground, and during extracurricular activities. The goal is to identify patterns and signs that may indicate SEN.

Educators should look for indicators such as difficulty with concentration, social interaction challenges, inconsistent academic performance, and behavioural changes. Regular observations over time can help distinguish between temporary issues and more persistent needs.

Teachers should document their observations in detail, noting specific behaviours, contexts, and any interventions attempted. This documentation provides valuable evidence for further assessment and helps inform the development of support plans.

Collaboration with Parents and Carers

Collaboration with parents and carers is essential for effective early identification and intervention. Parents and carers have unique insights into their child's development and behaviour, and their input can provide valuable context for educators. Building strong partnerships with families helps ensure that interventions are consistent and supportive across home and school environments.

Schools should establish regular communication channels with parents and carers, such as scheduled meetings, progress reports, and informal check-ins. Involving parents and carers in the assessment process and decision-making fosters a collaborative approach, ensuring that support plans are tailored to the student's needs and family circumstances.

Educators should also provide parents and carers with information and resources about SEN, including how to access further assessments and support services. Empowering families with knowledge and tools helps them advocate for their child's needs effectively.

Engaging with Primary School Feeder Settings

For secondary schools, engaging with primary school feeder settings is a vital aspect of early identification and intervention. Transition from primary to secondary school can be challenging for students with SEN, and seamless communication between schools ensures continuity of support.

Secondary schools should establish protocols for sharing information about incoming students with SEN. This includes detailed records of previous interventions, assessments, and support plans. Transition meetings involving primary and secondary school staff, parents, and the student can help facilitate a smooth handover and ensure that the student's needs are understood and addressed from the outset.

Secondary schools should also consider arranging visits and orientation sessions for incoming students with SEN. These activities help students familiarise themselves with the new environment, reducing anxiety and promoting a positive start to their secondary education.

Consider a secondary school that successfully implemented a preemptive identification and intervention strategy. The school used a combination of observational assessments, screening tools, and collaboration with primary feeder settings to identify students with potential SEN early. By establishing strong communication channels with parents and primary schools, the secondary school developed tailored support plans for each student. This proactive approach resulted in improved academic performance, reduced behavioural issues, and enhanced well-being for the students.

In another example, a primary school introduced regular training sessions for staff on identifying and supporting students with SEN. The school implemented a structured observation protocol and standardised checklists to ensure consistent identification of needs. By involving parents in the process and providing them with resources, the school created a supportive environment that facilitated early intervention and positive outcomes for students.

Practical Strategies for Early Identification

To further enhance early identification efforts, schools can implement specific strategies and practices. The preferred strategy is the use of a Graduated Approach, which involves a tiered approach to providing interventions based on the level of student need. This system allows for the early identification of students who may require additional support and provides a framework for delivering targeted interventions.

Another strategy is the implementation of universal screening programs. These programs involve regularly assessing all students to identify those who may be at risk of developing learning or behavioural difficulties. Screening tools can include academic assessments, behavioural checklists, and social-emotional surveys. The data collected from these screenings can help educators identify students who may benefit from further assessment or intervention.

Monitoring and Reviewing Interventions

Effective early identification and intervention require ongoing monitoring and review. Schools should establish processes for regularly evaluating the effectiveness of interventions and making necessary adjustments. This includes collecting data on student progress, gathering feedback from students, parents, and staff, and reviewing support plans.

Annual reviews and regular progress meetings provide opportunities to assess the impact of interventions, set new targets, and update support plans based on the student's evolving needs. By maintaining a dynamic and responsive approach, schools can ensure that students with SEN receive the support they need to thrive.

Chapter 4: Understanding Protected Characteristics

Protected characteristics are specific attributes that are safeguarded under the Equality Act 2010 to prevent discrimination and promote equality. In the context of education, these characteristics ensure that all students receive fair and equal treatment. The Act defines the following as protected characteristics:

Age: This applies mainly in employment contexts but is relevant in ensuring that students are not discriminated against based on their age, particularly in further education settings.

Disability: A broad category covering physical, sensory, intellectual, and mental health disabilities. The definition includes long-term conditions that substantially affect a person's ability to perform day-to-day activities.

Gender Reassignment: Protects individuals undergoing, planning to undergo, or who have undergone a process to change their gender. This characteristic ensures that students who are transitioning or have transitioned are supported and protected from discrimination.

Marriage and Civil Partnership: While primarily relevant in employment law, it ensures that students who are married or in civil partnerships are not discriminated against in FE settings.

Pregnancy and Maternity: Protects students who are pregnant, have recently given birth, or are breastfeeding, ensuring they are not unfairly treated or excluded from educational opportunities.

Race: Encompasses race, colour, nationality, and ethnic or national origins. This characteristic ensures that students from all racial backgrounds are treated equally and inclusively.

Religion or Belief: Protects individuals 'religious beliefs, philosophical beliefs, and lack of belief. Schools must accommodate students 'religious practices and avoid discrimination based on religious beliefs.

Sex: Ensures that students are not discriminated against based on their gender. This includes equal opportunities for male, female, and non-binary students.

Sexual Orientation: Protects students who are lesbian, gay, bisexual, or heterosexual, ensuring they are treated fairly regardless of their sexual orientation.

Disability as a Protected Characteristic

Disability, as defined by the Equality Act 2010, refers to a physical or mental impairment that has a substantial and long-term adverse effect on an individual's ability to perform normal day-to-day activities. This definition is intentionally broad to encompass a wide range of conditions, ensuring comprehensive protection for individuals with disabilities.

Physical Impairments: These include mobility impairments, visual and hearing impairments, and chronic illnesses such as diabetes and epilepsy. Physical impairments may require schools to make reasonable adjustments to the physical environment, such as providing wheelchair access or specialised equipment.

Mental Health Conditions: Conditions such as depression, anxiety, bipolar disorder, and schizophrenia are included under this characteristic. Schools need to provide appropriate support, including mental health services, counseling, and stress management programs.

Learning Disabilities and Difficulties: This category covers conditions such as dyslexia, autism spectrum disorder, ADHD, and intellectual disabilities. Schools must provide tailored educational support, including specialised teaching strategies and assistive technologies.

Long-term Conditions: The Act specifies that the impairment must be long-term, meaning it has lasted or is expected to last for at least 12 months. This includes conditions that may fluctuate or vary in severity over time.

Substantial Effect: The impairment must have a substantial effect on the individual's ability to carry out normal day-to-day activities. This includes activities such as walking, reading, writing, and social interaction.

By understanding the broad scope of disability as a protected characteristic, educators can better appreciate the diverse needs of students with disabilities and implement effective support strategies to ensure their full inclusion and participation in the educational environment.

In an educational context, understanding and accommodating protected characteristics is essential for creating an inclusive and equitable learning environment. Here are some practical examples:

Disability: A student with a hearing impairment might require the use of hearing aids and preferential seating in the classroom to ensure they can fully participate in lessons. The school might also provide sign language interpreters or captioning services for school assemblies and events.

Gender Reassignment: A transgender student undergoing gender reassignment might need access to appropriate facilities that align with their gender identity. The school should ensure that the student is addressed by their preferred name and pronouns and is supported throughout their transition.

Pregnancy and Maternity: A pregnant student might need adjustments to her schedule, such as additional breaks and a place to rest. The school should also provide accommodations for prenatal medical appointments and ensure that she can continue her studies without discrimination.

Race: A student from an ethnic minority background might face language barriers. The school could provide language support services, such as English as an Additional Language (EAL) programs, to help the student overcome these challenges and succeed academically.

Religion or Belief: A student who practices a particular religion may require accommodations for prayer times, dietary restrictions, or religious holidays. Schools should be flexible in allowing time and space for religious observance and should respect religious dress codes.

Sexual Orientation: A student who identifies as gay or lesbian should feel safe and supported in their school environment. This includes having access to resources such as LGBTQ+ support groups and ensuring that anti-bullying policies explicitly protect against harassment based on sexual orientation.

IMPACT ON STUDENTS AND REQUIRED ADJUSTMENTS

Understanding the impact of protected characteristics on students is essential for creating an inclusive educational environment. Recognising these impacts allows educators to make the necessary adjustments to support each student's unique needs, ensuring they can fully participate in school life and achieve their potential.

Impact on Students

Disability: Students with disabilities may face physical, sensory, cognitive, or emotional barriers to learning. For example, a student with a physical disability might struggle with accessing certain areas of the school or using standard classroom equipment. A student with a learning disability like dyslexia may find traditional reading and writing tasks challenging. These barriers can lead to feelings of frustration, low self-esteem, and disengagement if not appropriately addressed.

Gender Reassignment: Transgender students undergoing or having undergone gender reassignment may face social challenges, such as acceptance from peers and staff, and logistical issues, such as accessing appropriate facilities. Misgendering and lack of support can significantly impact their mental health and academic performance.

Pregnancy and Maternity: Pregnant students and young parents may struggle to balance their educational commitments with their health needs and parental responsibilities. This can lead to increased stress, absenteeism, and the potential for dropping out if adequate support is not provided.

Race: Students from ethnic minority backgrounds might experience racism, language barriers, and cultural misunderstandings. These challenges can affect their sense of belonging, self-identity, and academic performance. They may also face lower expectations from teachers and peers, impacting their motivation and achievement.

Religion or Belief: Students with specific religious beliefs may need to observe particular practices, such as prayer times, dietary restrictions, and dress codes. Failure to accommodate these needs can lead to feelings of exclusion and disrespect, negatively affecting their school experience and engagement.

Sexual Orientation: Students who identify as LGBTQ+ may face bullying, discrimination, and a lack of acceptance from peers and staff. This can result in mental health issues, such as anxiety and depression, and negatively impact their academic performance and overall well-being.

Required Adjustments

To address the unique needs of students with protected characteristics, schools must implement a variety of adjustments. These adjustments should be proactive, flexible, and tailored to the individual student.

Disability:

- **Physical Adjustments**: Ensuring the school environment is accessible by installing ramps, lifts, and accessible toilets. Providing specialised equipment, such as adapted desks and hearing aids, to facilitate learning.

- **Academic Support**: Implementing Individual Education Plans (IEPs) and providing tailored learning materials and assistive technologies. Offering additional support through teaching assistants and specialist educators.

Gender Reassignment:

- **Social Support**: Providing a supportive and inclusive environment where the student's chosen name and pronouns are respected. Offering counselling and peer support groups to help with the transition process.

- **Facility Access**: Ensuring access to appropriate changing rooms and toilets that align with the student's gender identity.

Pregnancy and Maternity:

- **Flexible Scheduling**: Allowing flexible timetables and breaks to accommodate health needs and parental responsibilities. Providing access to on-site childcare facilities or support for off-site childcare.

- **Health and Academic Support**: Offering tailored academic support and counselling to help manage stress and maintain academic progress.

Race:

- **Cultural Competence**: Training staff in cultural awareness and sensitivity to address and prevent racism and bias. Celebrating cultural diversity through curriculum content and school events.

- **Language Support**: Providing English as an Additional Language (EAL) programs and translation services to help students and their families overcome language barriers.

Religion or Belief:

- **Accommodation of Religious Practices**: Allowing time and space for prayer, respecting dietary restrictions in school meals, and permitting religious dress codes. Scheduling exams and important school events with consideration of religious holidays.

- **Inclusive Curriculum**: Incorporating diverse religious perspectives into the curriculum to foster understanding and respect among all students.

Sexual Orientation:

- **Anti-Bullying Policies**: Implementing and enforcing comprehensive anti-bullying policies that explicitly protect LGBTQ+ students. Providing training for staff and students on LGBTQ+ issues and creating a safe and supportive environment.

- **Support Services**: Offering access to LGBTQ+ support groups, counselling services, and resources to help students navigate their identities and experiences.

LEGAL IMPLICATIONS OF IGNORING PROTECTED CHARACTERISTICS

Ignoring the protected characteristics defined by the Equality Act 2010 can have serious legal implications for educational institutions. Schools and colleges have a legal duty to prevent discrimination and promote equality. Failure to do so can result in legal action and significant consequences.

Discrimination Claims: If a student or their family believes that the student has been discriminated against based on a protected characteristic, they can file a discrimination claim against the school. This can lead to legal proceedings and, if the claim is upheld, the school may be required to pay compensation and make changes to its policies and practices.

Investigations and Sanctions: Regulatory bodies, such as Ofsted, may conduct investigations into complaints of discrimination. If a school is found to be in breach of its legal duties under the Equality Act 2010, it can face sanctions, including fines and mandatory training for staff. The school's reputation can also suffer, affecting enrolment and community trust.

Compliance with EHC Plans: For students with disabilities, schools must comply with the provisions outlined in their Education, Health, and Care (EHC) plans. Ignoring or selectively implementing parts of an EHC plan can lead to legal challenges and complaints to the local authority. Schools are delegated the responsibility to provide the specified support and accommodations to ensure the student's needs are met.

Negative Impact on School Culture: Ignoring protected characteristics can create a hostile and non-inclusive school environment. This can lead to increased absenteeism, higher dropout rates, and lower academic performance among affected students. It also negatively impacts the overall school culture, making it less welcoming and supportive for all students.

Practical Implementation

Implementing these adjustments requires a coordinated effort across the school community. Teachers, support staff, administrators, and external professionals must work together to create a supportive and inclusive environment. Here are some steps for practical implementation:

Policy Development and Training: Schools should develop comprehensive policies that outline their commitment to supporting students with protected characteristics. Regular training sessions for staff on these policies and best practices for inclusion are essential.

Individualised Support Plans: Developing individualised support plans, such as IEPs[1] and IHP[2]s, ensures that each student's unique needs are met. These plans should be regularly reviewed and updated based on ongoing assessments and feedback.

Family and Community Engagement: Engaging with families and the broader community helps build a supportive network for students. Regular communication with parents and carers, as well as collaboration with local support organisations, enhances the support provided to students.

Monitoring and Evaluation: Schools should establish processes for monitoring the effectiveness of the adjustments and interventions implemented. Collecting data on student outcomes, gathering feedback from students and parents, and conducting regular reviews help ensure that support remains effective and relevant.

---

[1] IEP - individual education plan - may be called a OnePlan, passport, portfolio, profile or something similar in your school

[2] IHP - individual health plan - usually produced in conjunction with medical professionals

By understanding the impact of protected characteristics, making the necessary adjustments, and acknowledging the legal implications of non-compliance, schools can create an inclusive environment where all students feel valued, supported, and able to succeed.

PROMOTING AN INCLUSIVE ENVIRONMENT

Creating an inclusive environment is essential for ensuring that all students, regardless of their protected characteristics, feel valued, supported, and able to succeed. An inclusive school environment fosters respect, diversity, and equality, allowing every student to thrive. This section explores strategies for promoting inclusivity in educational settings.

School Policies and Leadership

Strong leadership and clear policies are the foundation of an inclusive school environment. School leaders must demonstrate a commitment to inclusivity and ensure that policies reflect this commitment.

Inclusive Policies: Schools should develop comprehensive policies that explicitly promote equality and inclusion. These policies should cover all aspects of school life, including admissions, behaviour, curriculum, and extracurricular activities. Policies should be regularly reviewed and updated to ensure they remain effective and relevant.

Leadership Commitment: School leaders must lead by example, promoting an inclusive culture through their actions and decisions. This includes addressing any instances of discrimination or exclusion promptly and effectively. Leaders should also ensure that all staff understand and adhere to the school's inclusivity policies.

Training and Professional Development: Providing ongoing training for staff on issues related to diversity, equity, and inclusion is crucial. Training should cover topics such as recognising and addressing unconscious bias, supporting students with protected characteristics, and implementing inclusive teaching practices. Regular professional development ensures that staff are equipped with the knowledge and skills to create an inclusive environment.

Curriculum and Teaching Practices

An inclusive curriculum and teaching practices are essential for promoting diversity and equality in the classroom.

Inclusive Curriculum: Schools should ensure that their curriculum reflects the diverse backgrounds and experiences of all students. This includes incorporating perspectives from different cultures, religions, and identities into lesson plans and materials. An inclusive curriculum helps students understand and appreciate diversity, fostering a sense of belonging and respect for others.

Differentiated Instruction: Teachers should use differentiated instruction to meet the diverse needs of their students. This involves adapting teaching methods and materials to ensure that all students can access the curriculum and participate fully in lessons. Strategies such as flexible grouping, varied assessment methods, and the use of assistive technologies can help accommodate different learning styles and abilities.

Student-Centred Learning: Promoting student-centred learning involves giving students a voice in their education. This can include involving them in setting learning goals, choosing topics of interest, and providing opportunities for self-assessment. Student-centred learning fosters engagement and ownership of learning, which is particularly important for students with protected characteristics.

School Culture and Environment

Creating a positive school culture and environment is key to fostering inclusivity.

Respect and Tolerance: Schools should cultivate a culture of respect and tolerance, where diversity is celebrated, and all students feel safe and valued. This includes implementing anti-bullying policies that specifically address discrimination based on protected characteristics and promoting positive behaviour through school-wide initiatives.

Student Involvement: Encouraging student involvement in promoting inclusivity helps build a supportive community. Schools can establish student councils, diversity committees, or peer mentoring programs that give students a platform to advocate for inclusivity and support their peers. Student-led initiatives can have a powerful impact on creating an inclusive environment.

Physical Environment: The physical environment of the school should be accessible and welcoming to all students. This includes ensuring that facilities are accessible to students with disabilities, providing quiet spaces for students who need them, and displaying materials that reflect the diversity of the school community.

Collaboration with Families and the Community

Engaging families and the broader community is essential for promoting inclusivity in schools.

Family Engagement: Schools should build strong partnerships with families, recognising them as key partners in their children's education. This includes regular communication with parents and carers, involving them in decision-making processes, and providing opportunities for them to contribute to school activities and events.

Community Partnerships: Schools can enhance their inclusivity efforts by partnering with local organisations and community groups. These partnerships can provide additional resources, support, and expertise, helping schools to better meet the needs of their diverse student population.

Cultural Competence: Developing cultural competence among staff and students helps build understanding and respect for different cultures and identities. This can be achieved through cultural awareness training, celebrating cultural events, and incorporating diverse cultural perspectives into the curriculum.

Regular monitoring and evaluation are crucial for ensuring that inclusivity efforts are effective and sustainable.

Data Collection and Analysis: Schools should collect and analyse data on student outcomes, participation, and well-being to identify any disparities or areas for improvement. This data can inform the development and refinement of inclusivity policies and practices.

Feedback Mechanisms: Providing opportunities for students, parents, and staff to give feedback on inclusivity efforts helps ensure that these efforts are meeting the needs of the school community. Schools can use surveys, focus groups, and suggestion boxes to gather input and identify areas for improvement.

Continuous Improvement: Inclusivity efforts should be viewed as an ongoing process. Schools should regularly review and update their policies, practices, and training programs to ensure they remain relevant and effective. Engaging in continuous improvement helps schools to adapt to changing needs and promote a culture of inclusivity.

Chapter 5: Implementing Support in the Classroom

Adaptive teaching is a flexible approach to instruction that ensures all students can achieve the same learning objectives, regardless of their individual needs and abilities. This approach emphasises the use of a variety of teaching methods and resources to accommodate different learning styles and needs within the same lesson. Adaptive teaching aims to create an inclusive classroom environment where all students can engage with the curriculum and achieve their full potential.

Understanding Student Needs

To effectively implement adaptive teaching, teachers must first understand the individual needs, strengths, and challenges of their students. This requires ongoing assessment and observation to identify each student's learning profile. Teachers should gather information from various sources, including student work, assessments, observations, and input from parents, carers, and other professionals.

Flexible Grouping

Flexible grouping is a key strategy in adaptive teaching. This approach allows students to work in different groups based on their learning needs, interests, or skill levels. These groups can be formed and reformed as needed to provide targeted instruction and support. For example, a teacher might create small groups for reading instruction based on students' reading levels or group students with similar interests for a project-based activity. Flexible grouping ensures that students receive the appropriate level of challenge and support.

Varied Instructional Methods

Using a variety of instructional methods can help meet the diverse needs of students. This might include whole-class instruction, small-group work, one-on-one support, and independent learning activities. Teachers should incorporate different teaching styles, such as visual, auditory, and kinaesthetic approaches, to cater to different learning preferences. For instance, visual learners may benefit from graphic organisers and visual aids, while kinaesthetic learners may engage more with hands-on activities.

Tiered Assignments (for Students Working Below Age-Related Expectations)

While adaptive teaching is the preferred approach, tiered assignments can be used for students working significantly below age-related expectations. Tiered assignments involve creating different levels of tasks that address the same learning objectives but vary in complexity. This allows students to work on tasks that are appropriate for their skill levels while still engaging with the core content. For example, in a history lesson, some students might work on a basic timeline of events, while others analyse primary source documents or write a detailed essay on a specific topic.

Learning Centres and Stations

Learning centres or stations are designated areas in the classroom where students can engage in different activities related to the lesson. Each station focuses on a specific skill or concept and allows students to work at their own pace. This approach provides opportunities for independent and collaborative learning and enables teachers to provide targeted support to small groups of students.

Ongoing Assessment and Feedback

Continuous assessment and feedback are essential components of adaptive teaching. Formative assessments, such as quizzes, observations, and student reflections, help teachers monitor student progress and adjust instruction as needed. Providing timely and specific feedback helps students understand their strengths and areas for improvement, guiding their learning process.

Use of Assistive Technology

Assistive technology can play a significant role in supporting students with SEND. It includes any device, software, or equipment that helps students overcome barriers to learning and participate fully in the classroom.

Types of Assistive Technology

Text-to-Speech Software: This technology converts written text into spoken words, helping students with reading difficulties, such as dyslexia, access written materials. Programs like Kurzweil 3000 and Read&Write can read aloud digital text from websites, documents, and e-books.

Speech-to-Text Software: Also known as voice recognition software, this technology allows students to dictate text into a computer or device. It is particularly useful for students with writing difficulties, enabling them to complete written assignments and communicate more effectively. Examples include DocsPlus and Texthelp (Read&Write).

Augmentative and Alternative Communication (AAC) Devices: AAC devices support students with communication challenges by providing alternative ways to express themselves. These devices range from simple picture boards to sophisticated speech-generating devices like Proloquo2Go and Picom AAC.

Graphic Organisers: Digital graphic organisers help students organise their thoughts and ideas visually. Tools like Inspiration and MindMeister enable students to create mind maps, flowcharts, and diagrams, aiding comprehension and planning.

Reading Pens: Reading pens, such as the C-Pen Reader, scan and read aloud printed text. They are portable and can be used by students with reading difficulties to access textbooks, worksheets, and other printed materials.

Integrating Assistive Technology in the Classroom

To effectively integrate assistive technology, teachers should consider the following steps:

Assessment and Selection: Collaborate with the SENCO, parents, and specialists to assess the student's needs and select the most appropriate assistive technology. Consider factors such as the student's learning profile, the tasks they need to perform, and the compatibility of the technology with existing systems.

Training and Support: Provide training for both students and staff on how to use the assistive technology effectively. Ongoing support and troubleshooting help ensure that the technology is used to its full potential.

Incorporating Technology into Lesson Plans: Plan lessons that incorporate assistive technology to enhance learning. For example, use text-to-speech software during reading activities or graphic organisers for writing assignments. Ensure that the technology is seamlessly integrated into the classroom routine.

Monitoring and Evaluation: Regularly monitor the student's progress and the effectiveness of the assistive technology. Gather feedback from the student, parents, and staff to make necessary adjustments and improvements.

Creating an Inclusive Classroom Culture

An inclusive classroom culture fosters a sense of belonging and respect for all students. It involves creating an environment where diversity is valued, and every student feels supported and included.

Building Positive Relationships

Building positive relationships with and among students is fundamental to creating an inclusive classroom. Teachers should strive to understand each student's background, interests, and strengths. Creating opportunities for students to share their experiences and learn about each other helps build a sense of community.

Promoting Respect and Empathy

Teaching respect and empathy is crucial for fostering an inclusive culture. Educators can incorporate lessons and activities that promote understanding and appreciation of diversity. For example, discussions on cultural differences, role-playing exercises, and collaborative projects can help students develop empathy and respect for others.

Setting High Expectations

Setting high expectations for all students is essential for an inclusive classroom. Teachers should communicate their belief in each student's potential and provide the support needed to achieve it. Celebrating successes and recognising effort reinforces a positive and inclusive mindset.

Encouraging Student Voice

Encouraging students to express their opinions and participate in decision-making empowers them and promotes inclusivity. Teachers can create forums, such as class meetings or suggestion boxes, where students can share their ideas and feedback. Involving students in setting classroom rules and goals also fosters a sense of ownership and responsibility.

Addressing Bias and Discrimination

Teachers must be vigilant in addressing any instances of bias, discrimination, or bullying in the classroom. Establishing clear policies and procedures for reporting and responding to such incidents is vital. Providing training on recognising and addressing bias helps create a safe and respectful learning environment.

Consider a secondary school where teachers implemented adaptive teaching and flexible grouping to support students with diverse learning needs. In a mathematics class, students were grouped based on their understanding of the current topic. Each group received tailored instruction and tasks suited to their skill level. This approach allowed all students to progress at their own pace and ensured that everyone received the appropriate level of challenge and support.

In another example, a primary school integrated assistive technology to support students with dyslexia. The school provided text-to-speech software and reading pens, enabling students to access written materials more easily. Teachers received training on how to incorporate these tools into their lessons, resulting in improved reading comprehension and increased confidence among students.

Teaching assistants (TAs) and support staff play a crucial role in implementing support in the classroom. They provide additional help to students with SEND, assist with adaptive teaching, and help create an inclusive learning environment.

Collaboration with Teachers

Effective collaboration between teachers and TAs is essential for providing consistent and coordinated support. Regular communication and planning sessions ensure that TAs are informed about lesson objectives, student needs, and specific strategies to be used. TAs can assist with small-group instruction, one-on-one support, and monitoring student progress.

Providing Individualised Support

TAs can provide targeted support to students with SEND, helping them access the curriculum and participate in classroom activities. This might include breaking down tasks into manageable steps, providing visual aids, or offering additional explanations and examples. TAs can also help implement assistive technology and support students in using these tools effectively.

Facilitating Social Interaction

TAs can help facilitate social interactions and promote inclusion among students. This might involve supporting group work, encouraging cooperative learning activities, and helping students develop social skills. TAs can also provide supervision and guidance during unstructured times, such as recess or lunch, to ensure that all students feel included and supported.

Monitoring and Feedback

TAs play a vital role in monitoring student progress and providing feedback to teachers. They can keep detailed records of student performance, behaviour, and engagement, helping to identify any areas of concern or improvement. Regular feedback sessions with teachers ensure that support strategies are adjusted as needed to meet the evolving needs of students.

Chapter 6: Making Reasonable Adjustments

The process of making reasonable adjustments begins with accurately identifying the specific needs of each student. This requires a thorough assessment of their strengths and challenges, considering both academic and non-academic aspects. Effective identification involves collaboration among teachers, SENCOs, parents, carers, and external professionals.

Comprehensive Assessment: Teachers should use a variety of assessment tools and strategies to gather detailed information about each student's needs. This may include formal assessments, observations, and input from parents and external specialists. Understanding the student's learning style, behavioural patterns, and social interactions is crucial for developing effective support strategies.

Holistic Approach: Consider both academic and non-academic needs. For instance, a student with mobility issues may require physical adjustments in the classroom, while a student with anxiety might need emotional support and stress management strategies. Addressing the whole child ensures that all aspects of their well-being are considered.

Continuous Monitoring: Needs can change over time, so regular monitoring and re-evaluation are essential. Ongoing assessments help track progress and identify any emerging issues that may require additional adjustments.

Physical Environment:

- *Accessibility*: Ensure the school environment is physically accessible to all students. This includes ramps, lifts, widened doorways, and accessible toilets. Classroom layouts should be arranged to allow easy movement for students with mobility aids.

- *Seating Arrangements*: Adjust seating plans to accommodate students with visual or hearing impairments, ensuring they can see the board and hear the teacher clearly. Provide seating options that cater to students who may need to move frequently or sit in specific postures.

Curriculum Delivery:

- *Differentiated Materials*: For students working well below age-related expectations, provide differentiated materials that match their learning levels while still engaging with the core content. This might include simplified texts, visual aids, and step-by-step instructions.

- *Multi-Sensory Approaches*: Use multi-sensory teaching methods to cater to different learning styles. Incorporate visual, auditory, and kinaesthetic activities to help students grasp concepts more effectively.

- *Pacing and Timing*: Adjust the pace of lessons to ensure all students can keep up. Provide additional time for tasks and allow breaks to prevent fatigue, especially for students with attention difficulties or medical conditions.

Assessment Methods:

- *Alternative Assessments*: Offer alternative assessment methods for students who struggle with traditional exams. This might include oral presentations, projects, or practical demonstrations that allow students to showcase their understanding in different ways.

- *Modified Exams*: Provide modified exam papers with larger print, simplified language, or additional instructions to make them accessible to students with specific needs. Allow the use of assistive technology during exams, such as text-to-speech software or word processors.

Balancing Individual Needs and Group Dynamics:

- *Inclusive Group Work*: Organise group activities that encourage collaboration and ensure all students can participate. Assign roles that play to each student's strengths and provide clear instructions and support to facilitate cooperation.

- *Positive Behaviour Support*: Implement strategies to support positive behaviour and manage any behavioural challenges. This might include clear rules, consistent routines, and positive reinforcement to create a supportive classroom environment.

Monitoring and Reviewing Adjustments:

- *Regular Reviews*: Conduct regular reviews of the adjustments in place to ensure they remain effective and relevant. This involves gathering feedback from students, parents, and staff, and making necessary changes based on this feedback.

- *Data Collection*: Collect and analyse data on student performance and engagement to evaluate the impact of the adjustments. Use this data to identify areas for improvement and adjust support strategies accordingly.

- *Student Involvement*: Involve students in the review process by seeking their input on the effectiveness of the adjustments and any additional support they might need. Empowering students to take an active role in their education fosters independence and self-advocacy.

Consider a secondary school that made significant adjustments to support a student with visual impairment. The school installed screen readers and magnification software on all computers and provided textbooks in Braille. Teachers received training on creating accessible materials and using assistive technology. These adjustments enabled the student to access the curriculum fully and participate in all classroom activities.

In another example, a primary school supported a student with autism by implementing a structured routine and visual schedules. The student had access to a quiet space for breaks and used a communication book to express their needs. The school also provided social skills training and facilitated peer support groups, creating an inclusive environment that promoted social interaction and reduced anxiety.

Making reasonable adjustments requires ongoing collaboration and a commitment to continuous improvement. Schools should work closely with parents, carers, and external professionals to ensure that support strategies are effective and comprehensive.

Team Approach: Foster a team approach where teachers, SENCOs, TAs, and other staff work together to support students with SEND. Regular team meetings and collaborative planning sessions help ensure that everyone is aligned and informed about each student's needs and progress.

Professional Development: Provide regular professional development opportunities for staff to enhance their understanding of SEND and effective support strategies. Training should cover topics such as adaptive teaching, assistive technology, and behaviour management.

Feedback and Reflection: Encourage a culture of feedback and reflection where staff, students, and parents can share their experiences and suggestions. Use this feedback to inform practice and drive continuous improvement.

Resource Allocation: Ensure that adequate resources are allocated to support the implementation of reasonable adjustments. This includes funding for assistive technology, training, and additional support staff.

Chapter 7: Normal Way of Working and Access Arrangements for Examinations

(SEE ALSO THE BOOK QFT 7: ASSESSMENT)

DEFINITION OF NORMAL WAY OF WORKING

The concept of "normal way of working" refers to the usual methods and strategies a student uses to complete tasks and demonstrate their understanding in the classroom. For students with special educational needs and disabilities (SEND), the normal way of working may include specific accommodations or support strategies that enable them to access the curriculum and perform at their best. These practices are established over time and are integral to the student's daily educational experience.

Establishing a student's normal way of working is crucial for making informed decisions about access arrangements for examinations. It ensures that the support provided during exams reflects the usual support the student receives in the classroom, thereby creating a fair and equitable assessment environment.

Types of Access Arrangements

Access arrangements are adjustments made to examination conditions to ensure that students with SEND are not disadvantaged. These arrangements are based on the student's normal way of working and are tailored to meet their specific needs. Some common types of access arrangements include:

Extra Time: Additional time is provided to students who require more time to process information, read questions, or complete answers due to a disability or learning difficulty. The amount of extra time is typically 25%, but it can be adjusted based on individual needs.

Readers and Scribes: A reader can be provided to read the exam questions and any necessary text to the student. A scribe can write down the student's dictated answers. These arrangements are often used for students with visual impairments, severe dyslexia, or physical disabilities that affect writing.

Modified Papers: Exam papers can be modified to meet the specific needs of students. This might include providing large print or Braille papers for visually impaired students or simplifying the language for students with significant cognitive impairments.

Assistive Technology: Students may use assistive technology such as word processors, text-to-speech software, or speech-to-text software during exams. This technology helps students with reading, writing, or communication difficulties to complete their exams effectively.

Rest Breaks: Supervised rest breaks can be provided to students who need to manage fatigue, pain, or anxiety. These breaks allow students to rest without losing examination time.

Separate Room: Some students may benefit from taking their exams in a separate room to reduce distractions and anxiety. This arrangement can be particularly helpful for students with ADHD, autism spectrum disorder, or severe anxiety. Separate room does not necessarily mean individual rooming.

Procedures for Applying Access Arrangements

Applying for access arrangements involves several steps, ensuring that the necessary support is documented and approved. The process typically includes the following:

Assessment and Evidence: Schools must gather evidence to support the need for access arrangements. This evidence can come from a variety of sources, including educational psychologists, medical professionals, and the school's SENCO. The assessment should clearly demonstrate how the student's disability or learning difficulty impacts their ability to perform under standard examination conditions.

Application Submission: Schools submit applications for access arrangements to the relevant examination boards. These applications must include detailed evidence of the student's normal way of working and the specific adjustments required. Each examination board has its own procedures and deadlines, so schools must be familiar with these requirements.

Approval and Implementation: Once approved, schools must ensure that the access arrangements are implemented effectively during examinations. This includes providing any necessary training for staff, arranging for the required resources, and making logistical arrangements such as booking separate rooms.

Ensuring Fairness in Assessments

The goal of access arrangements is to level the playing field for students with SEND, ensuring that they can demonstrate their knowledge and skills without being disadvantaged by their disabilities. However, it is essential to balance providing support with maintaining the integrity and standards of the assessment.

Consistency and Fairness: Access arrangements should be consistent with the student's normal way of working and should not provide an unfair advantage. Schools must ensure that the support provided is proportionate to the student's needs and aligns with the standard examination conditions as closely as possible.

Training and Awareness: All staff involved in administering exams must be trained in the specific access arrangements and understand their importance. This training ensures that staff can provide the necessary support and handle any issues that arise during the examination process.

Monitoring and Review: Regularly review the effectiveness of access arrangements and make adjustments as needed. This involves gathering feedback from students, parents, and staff, and monitoring exam performance to ensure that the arrangements are supporting students appropriately.

The Joint Council for Qualifications (JCQ) provides comprehensive guidelines for implementing access arrangements in examinations. These guidelines ensure standardised practices across different examination boards and educational institutions.

Regulations and Documentation: The JCQ publishes annual regulations that outline the requirements and procedures for access arrangements. Schools must stay updated with these regulations and ensure compliance. The guidelines provide detailed information on the types of evidence required, the application process, and the implementation of approved arrangements.

Centre Responsibilities: Schools and examination centres are responsible for ensuring that access arrangements are applied correctly and consistently. This includes maintaining accurate records of all arrangements, conducting assessments in line with JCQ requirements, and providing training for staff.

Monitoring and Compliance: The JCQ conducts audits and inspections to ensure that schools comply with the regulations. Non-compliance can result in sanctions and impact the school's ability to offer qualifications. Schools must be prepared for these audits and maintain thorough documentation to demonstrate compliance.

Consider a secondary school that effectively implemented access arrangements for a student with severe dyslexia. The student's normal way of working included using text-to-speech software and receiving extra time for assignments. For exams, the school provided the same text-to-speech software and 25% extra time. This arrangement allowed the student to process and understand the exam questions, resulting in improved performance and reduced anxiety.

In another example, a primary school supported a student with ADHD by arranging supervised rest breaks during exams. The student's normal way of working involved taking short breaks to manage concentration and hyperactivity. By incorporating rest breaks into the exam, the student could maintain focus and complete the exam more effectively.

Monitoring and Reviewing Access Arrangements

Effective implementation of access arrangements requires ongoing monitoring and review to ensure they continue to meet the students' needs.

Regular Reviews: Conduct regular reviews of access arrangements to ensure they remain appropriate and effective. This includes gathering feedback from students, parents, and staff, and making necessary adjustments based on this feedback.

Data Collection: Collect and analyse data on student performance and engagement during exams to evaluate the impact of the access arrangements. Use this data to identify areas for improvement and adjust support strategies accordingly.

Student Involvement: Involve students in the review process by seeking their input on the effectiveness of the access arrangements and any additional support they might need. Empowering students to take an active role in their education fosters independence and self-advocacy.

By understanding and implementing the concept of normal way of working, applying appropriate access arrangements, and adhering to JCQ guidelines, schools can ensure that students with SEND have the support they need to succeed in examinations. This approach promotes fairness and equity, helping all students demonstrate their true abilities.

Chapter 8: Supporting Students with Medical Needs

UNDERSTANDING MEDICAL NEEDS IN AN EDUCATIONAL CONTEXT

Supporting students with medical needs is crucial to ensuring that they have equal access to education and can participate fully in school life. Medical needs can range from chronic illnesses and physical disabilities to temporary conditions and mental health issues. Each student's situation is unique, requiring tailored support and accommodations to meet their specific needs.

Students with medical needs may require adjustments to the school environment, personalised health care plans, and ongoing collaboration between educators, healthcare providers, and families. Addressing these needs effectively helps prevent disruptions to the student's education and promotes their overall well-being.

Types of Medical Needs

Chronic Illnesses: Conditions such as asthma, diabetes, epilepsy, and cystic fibrosis require regular monitoring and management. Students may need medication administration during school hours and access to emergency care plans.

Physical Disabilities: Students with physical disabilities may need physical accommodations, such as wheelchair access, modified seating, and assistive devices. They may also require support with mobility and daily activities.

Mental Health Conditions: Conditions such as anxiety, depression, ADHD, and eating disorders can significantly impact a student's ability to focus, engage, and succeed in school. Support may include counseling, stress management strategies, and accommodations for exams and assignments.

Temporary Conditions: Injuries or short-term illnesses may require temporary adjustments, such as modified physical education activities or permission to rest during the school day.

Creating Individual Healthcare Plans

Individual Healthcare Plans (IHPs) are essential for outlining the specific support and accommodations needed for students with medical needs. IHPs are developed collaboratively, involving the student, their parents or carers, healthcare professionals, and school staff. These plans ensure that everyone involved understands the student's needs and the steps required to support them effectively.

Developing an IHP: The process begins with a comprehensive assessment of the student's medical condition and its impact on their school life. The IHP should include detailed information about the condition, required medications, emergency procedures, and any necessary accommodations. It should also outline the roles and responsibilities of school staff in managing the student's needs.

Components of an IHP: Key elements of an IHP include:

- *Medical Information*: Details of the medical condition, including symptoms, triggers, and treatment.

- *Medication Management*: Instructions for administering medication, including dosage, timing, and storage. Procedures for handling medication emergencies.

- *Emergency Procedures*: Clear guidelines for managing medical emergencies, including contact information for healthcare providers and emergency contacts.

- *Accommodations*: Specific adjustments to the school environment, curriculum, and assessments to support the student's participation and success.

- *Monitoring and Review*: Plans for regular monitoring of the student's condition and periodic review of the IHP to ensure it remains effective and up-to-date.

Training Staff to Support Medical Needs

Training school staff is crucial to effectively supporting students with medical needs. Staff must be equipped with the knowledge and skills to implement IHPs, administer medication, and respond to medical emergencies. Training should be ongoing and updated regularly to ensure that all staff remain competent and confident in their roles.

Initial Training: When a student with medical needs joins the school or receives a new diagnosis, initial training sessions should be conducted. These sessions should cover the specific medical condition, the student's IHP, and general procedures for managing medical needs in the school setting.

Ongoing Training: Regular refresher courses and updates are necessary to keep staff informed about any changes to the student's condition or treatment plan. Ongoing training ensures that all staff, including new hires and substitutes, are prepared to support students with medical needs.

Emergency Response Training: Specific training on handling medical emergencies is vital. Staff should know how to recognise symptoms of a medical crisis, administer first aid, and follow the emergency procedures outlined in the IHP. Regular drills and practice scenarios can help staff respond quickly and effectively in real-life situations.

Legal Obligations and Best Practices

Schools have a legal duty to support students with medical needs, ensuring that they have access to education and are not discriminated against due to their medical conditions. Key legislation and guidance include the Equality Act 2010 and the statutory guidance for supporting pupils at school with medical conditions.

Equality Act 2010: Under this Act, schools must make reasonable adjustments to avoid disadvantaging students with disabilities, including those with medical needs. This includes providing necessary accommodations and support to ensure that these students can participate fully in school life.

Statutory Guidance: The Department for Education's statutory guidance outlines schools' responsibilities for supporting students with medical conditions. It emphasises the importance of developing IHPs, training staff, and creating an inclusive school environment. Schools must comply with this guidance to meet their legal obligations and promote the well-being of students with medical needs.

Best Practices:

- **Inclusive Policies**: Develop and implement policies that promote the inclusion and support of students with medical needs. These policies should be communicated clearly to all staff, students, and parents.

- **Collaboration**: Foster strong partnerships with healthcare providers, parents, and external agencies to ensure comprehensive support for students.

- **Communication**: Maintain open lines of communication with students and their families to keep them informed about their care and any changes to their support plans.

- **Confidentiality**: Respect the privacy of students with medical needs by handling their information confidentially and sharing it only with those directly involved in their care.

Consider a primary school that successfully supported a student with diabetes. The school worked with the student's parents and healthcare team to develop a comprehensive IHP. Staff received training on monitoring blood sugar levels, administering insulin, and recognising signs of hypoglycaemia. The school also provided the student with a private area for blood sugar checks and insulin administration, ensuring that the student could manage their condition discreetly and effectively.

In another example, a secondary school supported a student with severe asthma by implementing a detailed IHP that included emergency procedures and daily medication management. The school trained staff on how to use the student's inhaler and recognise asthma triggers. They also adapted the physical education curriculum to accommodate the student's condition, allowing them to participate safely in physical activities.

Monitoring and Reviewing IHPs

Regular monitoring and review of IHPs are essential to ensure they remain effective and relevant. Schools should establish processes for ongoing assessment and feedback, involving all stakeholders in the review process.

Regular Check-Ins: Schedule regular check-ins with the student, parents, and healthcare providers to review the IHP and make any necessary adjustments. These check-ins can be part of parent-teacher conferences or separate meetings dedicated to discussing the student's medical needs.

Annual Reviews: Conduct formal annual reviews of the IHP to evaluate its effectiveness and update it based on any changes in the student's condition or treatment plan. Annual reviews provide an opportunity to reflect on the past year's successes and challenges and plan for the future.

Data Collection: Collect and analyse data on the student's health, academic performance, and engagement to assess the impact of the IHP. Use this data to identify areas for improvement and adjust support strategies accordingly.

Student Involvement: Involve students in the review process by seeking their input on the effectiveness of the IHP and any additional support they might need. Empowering students to take an active role in managing their medical needs fosters independence and self-advocacy.

Chapter 9: Understanding and Applying Key Concepts

In the context of education, understanding the differences between equity, equality, inclusion, seclusion, and integration is crucial for creating an environment where all students can thrive. These terms are often used interchangeably, but they have distinct meanings and implications for educational practice.

Equality: Equality involves treating everyone the same, ensuring that all students have access to the same resources, opportunities, and support. While this approach aims to promote fairness, it does not account for the diverse needs and starting points of individual students. In practice, equality might mean providing all students with the same textbook, regardless of their reading levels or learning styles.

Equity: Equity, on the other hand, involves recognising and addressing the unique needs of each student to ensure fair outcomes. This approach acknowledges that some students may require additional or different resources and support to achieve the same level of success as their peers. Equity might involve providing additional tutoring for students who are struggling, offering assistive technology for students with disabilities, or adjusting teaching methods to cater to diverse learning styles.

Inclusion: Inclusion is the practice of ensuring that all students, regardless of their abilities or backgrounds, are fully integrated into the school community. This involves creating a supportive and accessible environment where every student feels valued and can participate in all aspects of school life. Inclusive education is proactive and seeks to remove barriers to learning and participation, promoting a sense of belonging for all students.

Seclusion: Seclusion refers to the practice of isolating students, typically for behavioural management or safety reasons. While sometimes necessary, seclusion should be used sparingly and only when absolutely required, as it can have negative impacts on a student's social and emotional well-being. Schools should have clear policies and procedures for the use of seclusion, ensuring that it is only used as a last resort and for the shortest time possible.

Integration: Integration involves placing students with special educational needs (SEN) or disabilities in mainstream classrooms. While this approach aims to bring students together, it does not always guarantee that they will receive the support they need to succeed. True integration requires thoughtful planning and the provision of appropriate resources and support to ensure that all students can participate fully in the learning process.

Diversity: Diversity refers to the recognition and valuing of differences among individuals. In an educational context, diversity encompasses various dimensions such as race, ethnicity, gender, age, disability, sexual orientation, religion, and socio-economic status. Embracing diversity involves creating a learning environment that respects and celebrates these differences, fostering a culture of acceptance and understanding.

Exclusion: Exclusion involves removing a student from a regular educational setting, either temporarily or permanently. This can occur as a disciplinary measure or when a student's needs cannot be met within the current setting. Exclusion can have significant negative impacts on a student's educational outcomes and well-being. Schools should seek to avoid exclusion by providing adequate support and interventions to address the underlying issues.

Equity in Practice:

- **Tailored Support**: Provide additional resources and support tailored to the needs of individual students. For example, offer specialised tutoring, assistive technology, or differentiated instruction based on the student's unique requirements.

- **Proactive Identification**: Regularly assess and identify the specific needs of students to provide timely and effective interventions.

Inclusive Education:

- **Accessible Environment**: Ensure that the school environment is physically and socially accessible to all students. This includes ramps, elevators, and accessible toilets, as well as fostering an inclusive school culture.

- **Universal Design for Learning (UDL)**: Implement UDL principles to create flexible learning environments that can accommodate individual learning differences. This approach benefits all students by providing multiple means of representation, engagement, and expression.

Addressing Seclusion and Integration:

- **Positive Behaviour Support**: Use positive behaviour support strategies to reduce the need for seclusion. Implement proactive measures to address behavioural issues and promote positive interactions.

- **Supportive Integration**: Ensure that students with SEN or disabilities placed in mainstream classrooms receive the necessary support. This might include co-teaching arrangements, the presence of teaching assistants, and access to specialised resources.

Promoting Diversity:

- **Culturally Relevant Curriculum**: Integrate diverse perspectives and content into the curriculum to reflect the backgrounds and experiences of all students. This helps students see themselves represented and promotes respect for different cultures and identities.

- **Celebrating Diversity**: Organise events and activities that celebrate cultural diversity, such as international days, festivals, and guest speakers. These events foster a sense of community and appreciation for diversity.

- **Preventative Measures**: Implement early intervention strategies to address behavioural and academic issues before they escalate. Provide counselling, mentoring, and additional academic support to help students succeed within the mainstream setting.

- **Reintegration Plans**: If exclusion occurs, develop comprehensive reintegration plans to support the student's return to the regular educational setting. This includes ongoing monitoring, support, and adjustments to address any remaining barriers.

Chapter 10: School Trips and Inclusive Planning

ENSURING INCLUSION ON SCHOOL TRIPS

School trips are valuable educational experiences that provide students with opportunities to learn outside the classroom, develop social skills, and build memories. It is essential to ensure that students with special educational needs and disabilities (SEND) can participate fully in these experiences. Schools have a legal and ethical obligation to include all students in school trips or provide suitable alternative arrangements.

Planning and Preparation: Inclusive school trips require thorough planning and preparation to accommodate the diverse needs of all students. This involves considering the destination, activities, transportation, and accommodations to ensure accessibility and safety.

Risk Assessments: Conduct comprehensive risk assessments for each trip, identifying potential hazards and challenges for students with SEND. The risk assessment should include:

- *Accessibility*: Evaluate the accessibility of the destination, including pathways, entrances, restrooms, and activity areas. Ensure that any required mobility aids or support services are available.

- *Medical Needs*: Plan for the medical needs of students, including medication management, emergency procedures, and the availability of first aid. Ensure that staff are trained to handle medical emergencies and that medical supplies are readily accessible.

- *Supervision and Support*: Determine the appropriate level of supervision and support required for students with SEND. This may include assigning additional staff or volunteers to provide one-on-one support or assist with specific needs.

Inclusive Activities: Choose activities that all students can participate in, or provide alternatives that are equally engaging and educational. Ensure that students with SEND are not excluded from any part of the trip due to their disabilities.

Communication with Parents and Carers: Engage in open and ongoing communication with the parents and carers of students with SEND. Discuss the details of the trip, including the planned activities, accommodations, and any specific needs their child may have. Involve parents and carers in the planning process to ensure that their concerns are addressed and that they feel confident about their child's participation.

Alternative Arrangements

If it is not feasible to include a student with SEND in a particular school trip, schools should arrange an alternative trip or activity for everyone that provides a similar educational experience. This ensures that the student does not miss out on valuable learning opportunities.

Equitable Alternatives: Plan alternative trips or activities that are equally engaging and educational, considering the student's interests and needs. Ensure that the alternative experience aligns with the learning objectives of the original trip.

A primary school planned a trip to a nature reserve, ensuring that all paths were accessible and that there were rest areas for students with mobility issues. The school arranged for a medical professional to accompany the trip, provided additional supervision for students with specific needs, and planned inclusive activities that all students could enjoy.

In another example, a secondary school organised a visit to a science museum. For a student with severe allergies, the school coordinated with the museum to ensure that no allergens were present and provided an alternative, allergen-free activity area. The school also conducted a thorough risk assessment and trained staff on how to respond to allergic reactions, ensuring the student's safety and inclusion.

Monitoring and Reviewing Inclusion on School Trips

Regularly review the inclusion policies and practices for school trips to ensure they remain effective and relevant. This involves gathering feedback from students, parents, and staff, and making necessary adjustments based on this feedback.

Regular Reviews: Conduct formal reviews of school trip policies and procedures to evaluate their effectiveness. Use these reviews to identify areas for improvement and update practices to enhance inclusion.

Feedback Mechanisms: Provide opportunities for students, parents, and staff to share their experiences and suggestions for improving inclusion on school trips. Use this feedback to inform future planning and decision-making.

About the Author

Abigail Hawkins – The Driving Force Behind Inclusive Education

With 30 years of experience, Abigail Hawkins stands as a seasoned and passionate SENCO, renowned for her commitment to advancing Special Educational Needs (SEN) provisions. As the founder of SENDCO Solutions and SENsible SENCO CIC, Abigail leverages her extensive expertise to offer invaluable support and guidance to educators and schools nationwide.

A Champion for All Learners

Abigail's vast experience spans a diverse range of subjects, addressing the needs of students from toddlers to adults. Her practical approach to SEN issues is underscored by a wealth of consultancy work, where she collaborates with leading software and product companies to pioneer innovative tools for SEN support. Her efforts extend to designing and delivering teaching assistant apprenticeship and master's degree programs, as well as authoring several books and resources on SEN and exclusions. Additionally, Abigail provides comprehensive support to schools through detailed reviews, targeted training sessions, and ongoing consultancy to ensure the effective implementation of SEN strategies.

Leading a Thriving Network

As the founder of a support network that empowers nearly 13,000 SENCOs, Abigail is dedicated to fostering connections and sharing vital resources. Her impactful tenure as the Chair of Governors for three schools in the East Midlands highlights her unwavering commitment to educational leadership.

Pioneering Beyond Traditional Channels

Abigail's influence transcends traditional educational frameworks. During the challenging lockdown periods, she was a key figure in hosting a series of SEN webinars that reached a global audience exceeding 60,000 viewers. Embracing modern communication methods, she also manages a successful YouTube channel, making SEN-related information both accessible and engaging.

A Relentless Advocate for Inclusive Education

Abigail's non-nonsense, hands-on approach enables her to make a significant impact in the lives of countless students, educators, and schools. Her steadfast dedication to inclusive education remains evident through her continuous efforts to promote and implement effective SEN strategies.

Becoming a subscriber to SENsible SENCo offers a wealth of advantages designed to support and enhance your role as an SEN professional. As a member, you will gain:

- **Exclusive Access to Resources**: Unlock a treasure trove of expertly curated materials, including guides, templates, and best practice strategies tailored specifically for SEN coordinators and educators.

- **Cutting-Edge Insights**: Stay ahead with the latest developments in SEN research, policy updates, and innovative teaching methods through our regularly updated content and newsletters.

- **Professional Development**: Benefit from comprehensive training modules, webinars, and workshops that provide valuable CPD opportunities, helping you to refine your skills and knowledge.

- **Community Support**: Join a vibrant community of like-minded professionals, sharing experiences, advice, and support through our forums and networking events.

These QFT booklets have been distributed to subscribers as an online version and they can easily access the videos that accompany. www.sensiblesenco.org.uk

Printed in Great Britain
by Amazon

51664469R00051